SHIRE NATURAL HISTORY

THE RABBIT

MICHAEL LEACH

CONTENTS

Cover: *Young rabbits inside the warren.*

Series editor: Jim Flegg.

Copyright © 1989 by Michael Leach. First published 1989.
Number 39 in the Shire Natural History series. ISBN 0 7478 0021 9.

Printed in Great Britain by C. I. Thomas & Sons (Haverfordwest) Ltd, Press Buildings, Merlins Bridge, Haverfordwest, Dyfed.

Introduction

The rabbit (*Oryctolagus cuniculus*) has a well established identity in western folklore, with a popular image as a lovable defenceless animal ill-equipped to face the dangers that surround it. In reality it is aggressive, adaptable and sturdy. Rabbits can survive in a wide variety of habitats, often under the most difficult conditions. Although they feature prominently in the diet of many predators, their population is maintained by a high breeding rate. Along with rats and mice, rabbits are amongst the most successful mammals in the world.

Originally rabbits were confined to south-west Europe and north-west Africa. For a variety of reasons, ranging from pure sentimentality to the need for a readily available meat supply, rabbits have been introduced to North and South America, South Africa, Australia, New Zealand and many other countries. With their broad diet and adaptable nature, rabbits thrived in these countries, sometimes multiplying to the point where they are a serious economic threat to agriculture.

Lagomorphs ('hare-shaped' animals: rabbits and hares) are at least fifty million years old. Fossil remains have been found from the Eocene period onwards and 44 member species can be found throughout the world with the exceptions of dense rain forest, polar regions and some of the more remote islands. The European rabbit is the ancestor of all varieties of pet and domestic rabbits. The lop-eared, dwarf and giant varieties like the Flemish have all originated by selective breeding from the same species.

Man has an ambivalent attitude towards the rabbit. It is condemned as an agricultural and horticultural pest, being hunted for its fur and commercially farmed for its meat. On the other hand it is the hero of many children's stories, such as those of Brer Rabbit, Peter Rabbit and *Watership Down*. Rabbits are also adored, and abused, in garden hutches everywhere, often being the first introduction that many people have to keeping and looking after animals. The life of the wild rabbit extends much beyond either of these images, and is worthy of respect and detailed study.

History

Rabbits originate from the western Mediterranean, particularly Morocco and Spain. They were introduced into Britain during the twelfth century AD. The first rabbits were kept in captivity to provide meat and fur, there being no comparable native species apart from the hare. It must have been difficult to cage these animals using only woven fence panels and ditches and soon rabbits escaped and established wild breeding colonies. With large tracts of forest, Britain was not ideal for rabbits, so they first colonised sand dunes and other areas where the vegetation was not dense. In addition, predators such as wolves, wildcats and eagles would have soon noticed the appearance of this new prey species.

At first rabbits were known as coneys and the word 'rabbit' was used only for their young. They were rare and regarded as delicacies for royal banquets. Live rabbits were often included in dues brought from estates loyal to the throne. During this transportation many must have escaped, helping to increase their range considerably. By the late thirteenth century records show that rabbits had become an agricultural pest in some areas, though elsewhere they were still rare and much prized. 'Warreners' were employed to protect the rabbits against attack from humans and animals. In the fourteenth century a group of poachers was excommunicated for stealing rabbits from a Somerset estate. The risk was worthwhile, as at that time rabbits could be sold for up to sixpence each. As this was a considerable sum of money, rabbits must have been seen as a great luxury.

Over the next four hundred years rabbits extended their range and colonised most of mainland Britain, often moving into areas where forests had been cleared. However, the population in Britain remained relatively constant until the middle of the nineteenth century, when,

1. *The Normans introduced the rabbit into England in the twelfth century and tried to keep them in fenced enclosures.*

for three basic reasons, their numbers began to increase dramatically. Firstly, more than four thousand Acts of Enclosure were passed to define land boundaries, which resulted in hedgerow planting on a massive scale, completely changing the landscape in parts of Britain. The inter-connecting network of hedgerows provided the rabbits with shelter and the opportunity to build warrens in loosened soil. Secondly, the agricultural revolution with its new techniques and inventions greatly increased the production of cereal crops, particularly in winter. This provided the rabbits with a ready-made and easily accessible food supply. Finally, improvements in firearms led to the development of the shooting estate at about the same time and game preservation became a major concern. In an attempt to protect pheasants, partridges and grouse any animal that was considered to be potentially carnivorous was killed. Foxes, stoats, weasels, pine martens and birds of prey were trapped, poisoned and shot on a scale not seen before or since. The disappearance of these major predators allowed rabbits to multiply rapidly. When gamekeeping entered a more enlightened age much of the killing ended but many species of pre-

dators never returned to their former ranges. Rabbit populations increased dramatically and the animal soon became a major agricultural pest.

During the Second World War the campaign to control rabbits was temporarily relaxed and the population reached numbers that were unimaginable a century before, even though many more were being eaten because of the shortage of other meat. By 1950 it was estimated that rabbits destroyed £50 million worth of crops a year. All attempts to reduce their numbers were unsuccessful: their destruction in large numbers had no perceptible effect. However, the fate of the rabbits had been determined in 1896.

In Uruguay a viral disease was discovered and given the name *Myxomatosis cuniculus*; it was harmless to its natural host, the forest rabbit. In 1952 a retired French doctor infected a pair of European rabbits with the myxoma virus and released them west of Paris. As the virus originated in South America the European species had no natural resistance to it. The virus causes swelling of the eyelids and base of the ears. In later stages the animal cannot see or hear, becomes totally disorientated and eventually dies. The virus is mainly transmitted by the

3

rabbit flea (*Spilopsyllus cuniculus*). These readily move from animal to animal and cross-infect with bites. In the densely populated warrens myxomatosis spread at an astonishing rate across mainland Europe. The first British record was in August 1953 in Kent, possibly as the result of the intentional release of infected rabbits. Once the effects were known many more such animals were imported and introduced into other parts of Britain. Myxomatosis is a particularly distressing disease and there was a public outcry over its use as a biological control. An amendment to the 1954 Pests Act was passed to make the introduction of myxomatosis illegal. But this did no more than slow the release of infected rabbits.

The disease spread as rapidly in Britain as it had in Europe, with terrible consequences. Although a small number contracted the virus and survived, within five years around 96 per cent of the rabbits in Britain had died. The deaths were on such a large scale that the Army was called in to move the corpses, as they posed a health hazard. No rabbit colony remained uninfected. Myxomatosis is now well established throughout Britain and for the time being prevents another resurgence of rabbits. Every now and then it erupts locally and wipes out most of the rabbits in small areas. But quickly other rabbits move in and recolonise. There is evidence that rabbits are developing a degree of resistance to myxomatosis, but it is far from complete immunity. Some rabbits now spend less time in the restrictive tunnels making up warrens and even breed above ground, which slows down the transfer of fleas.

The rabbit

The order Lagomorpha is split into two families, with rabbits and hares forming the larger group and fourteen species of pika making up the smaller. For a long time lagomorphs were grouped with rodents, then in 1912 they were reclassified as a separate order since they have several distinct features. The most obvious difference is that the lagomorphs have two pairs of upper incisors. One pair, known as the peg teeth, grows immediately behind the much larger, chisel-shaped, main incisors. Unlike the teeth of rodents, all those of the lagomorphs are rootless and grow continuously throughout their lives, which compensates for wear caused by eating tough vegetation.

Rabbits and hares have long, slit-like nostrils which they can open and close by retracting a fold of skin. When the nostrils are fully open, extremely sensitive pads are exposed, giving these animals a very acute sense of smell. Faced with a formidable array of predators, rabbits are well equipped to sense potential danger. Their ears are long and concave, capable of detecting and pinpointing sound very quickly, and can be rotated independently giving directional and

2. *In the late stages of myxomatosis infected rabbits are totally unaware of their surroundings and do not attempt to run off if a predator approaches.*

3. *Grooming takes place several times a day, particularly in the early evening. Rabbits clean themselves by scratching with the hind legs and then licking. Face and ears are cleaned with the forefeet, using the same action as a cat.*

accurate hearing. Their eyes are set high up on the side of the skull for maximum angle of view, which extends through 270 degrees.

The sexes are similar but the male, known as the buck, has a broader head and weighs more than the doe. A fully grown male rabbit has a maximum weight of 2000 grams and measures up to 40 cm long.

The coat is normally a grey-brown colour, but it can vary from sandy yellow to black and every colour in between. The underside of the animal is almost white although some individuals may be totally black (melanistic) or, occasionally, ginger (erythristic). Rabbits moult once a year, starting in March; the moult begins on the face and slowly spreads along the back and over the rest of the body. The growth of warm sub-surface fur is not completed until about October, in preparation for the cold months ahead.

Rabbits are often confused with hares but there are major differences. Both brown and mountain hares are larger than rabbits, and they have longer ears which are black-tipped. When they are running, the tail of the hare looks brown while that of the rabbit, which is curled up towards its body, shows its distinctly white underside. Rabbits move at any speed by putting their front legs down together and then hopping forward with their hind legs, also together. By comparison, the hare runs rather than hops. Relative to body size, the legs of a hare are much longer than those of a rabbit.

SIGNS

Rabbits can be found in a wide diversity of habitats, from sand dunes and moorland to arable land and golf courses. But seeing them is not always easy. In agricultural areas, where they are treated as pests and regularly hunted, rabbits are very wary of man. In urban parks, where they are almost encouraged as attractions, they may be much more approachable, although they are never tame.

If rabbits are present the most obvious indications are warren entrance holes. These are usually at the bottom of hedgerows, bushes or other vegetation but may sometimes be found in open ground. The entrance is 15-20 cm in

5

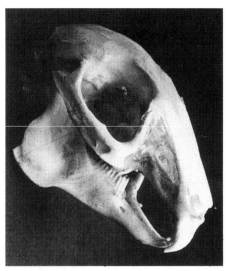

4. Rabbit skull, showing the characteristic gap between the incisors and molars known as the diastema.

occupied. Rabbit droppings are dark brown and almost spherical, with a diameter of around 10 mm. Generally they are darker than hare droppings but this is variable and depends upon the type of food supply. Researchers have used the density of pellets per hectare to estimate the population of rabbits in a warren. This is easy to estimate as rabbits pass approximately 360 pellets a day.

The footprints of rabbits are distinctive. They have hair on the underside of their feet to help grip at high speed and this hair softens the edges of the prints. The small forelegs have five toes and leave a tidy round print while the powerful hind legs leave a longer mark showing four toes. The hind feet leave a print measuring about 4 cm long and 2.5 cm wide. When the rabbit is moving slowly these tracks are slightly behind those of the forefeet but when it is running the stronger back legs frequently overtake the forelegs and the larger prints are then left in front. It is therefore possible to estimate the speed of an animal by looking at the relative position of the prints. Well used rabbit runs between the warren and favourite feeding grounds can be found by looking for snags of fur caught on fence wire or low in hedges. These snags are collected by birds to provide nest lining.

Like many species of mammal, rabbits use roadside verges as feeding grounds. In areas of intensive agriculture where monoculture reduces the choice of food, untended verges offer an attractive diversity of plants. Rabbits have long exploited this environment and an observant driver can often see them feeding just a metre or so from speeding traffic. At night, when they are caught in headlights, their eyes shine pink as light reflects off the tapetum, a reflective layer at the back of the eye that helps the rabbit to see in low light conditions. Road traffic accounts for a considerable percentage of casualties, young rabbits being particularly at risk as they lack experience. Dead rabbits form a major part of

diameter and, if it is in use, the soil in the hole will be smooth from the constant brushing of fur. Around the warren the grass will be close-cropped by grazing animals. As well as being a food source, this also has the advantage of giving the rabbits a clear view of their surroundings when first leaving the burrow. Tree saplings and fallen branches are often stripped as rabbits will eat tree bark. Their distinctive double-toothed scratches can be seen on the wood beneath. No other bark-stripping animal leaves these grooves except the hare. There may also be shallow scrapes in the soil where they have dug for edible roots. Larger scrapes can be seen where a rabbit has built a temporary ground nest, called a form. These are normally used only for a short time and can be in either open land or deep vegetation.

Fresh droppings are an obvious indication of rabbits. Because of the low nutritional value of their food, rabbits eat large quantities and therefore produce a lot of waste. Droppings can be left anywhere within their range but latrines are regularly used to mark colonial boundaries. Droppings are left on the edge of territories to act as scent marks. Latrines may be used by any rabbit from the warren and may contain a considerable amount of faecal matter, signalling to potential intruders that the area is

5. *Rabbit droppings.*

6. *Hind footprint.*

7. *Rabbit fur caught on a twig.*

8 (above left). *Tawny owl with young rabbit prey.*

9 (above right). *Foxes are amongst the most efficient and widespread predators on rabbits.*

10 (below). *Ferrets are often trained to drive rabbits out of a warren and into nets.*

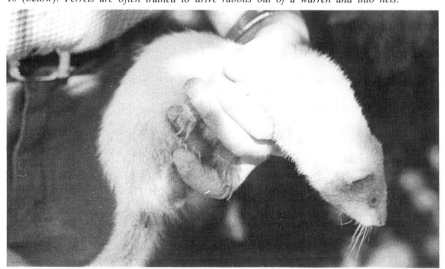

11. Rabbits form a major part of the diet of the buzzard, which will catch live rabbits as well as eating dead ones.

the diet of scavengers, and birds such as magpies and crows have learned that roads are profitable hunting grounds, quickly finding and disposing of corpses.

PREDATORS

In captivity rabbits may live up to ten years, but in the wild their life expectancy is not likely to exceed three years. If they are not killed by disease, they fall prey to an array of predators that live around them. From the first moments of life rabbits are vulnerable. Inside the nursery den they may be taken by weasels, which are small enough to enter the warren and find the young by smell. Badgers will dig out young rabbits from the more shallow nurseries. The highest mortality rate occurs immediately after the rabbit kittens leave the warren for the first time. During the first few months of life they lack the skill and co-ordination necessary to keep out of danger. When an adult is attacked it can fight back with a series of powerful kicks from its hind legs. It can also inflict deep bites with its long sharp incisors. Young rabbits cannot defend themselves so effectively and, being smaller, can be taken by a wider range of

predators. Owls, weasels and domestic cats readily hunt young rabbits but are not strong enough to cope with a healthy adult animal. Stoats, foxes, polecats and buzzards are the main predators on adult rabbits. There is also localised hunting by golden eagles, wildcats, ravens and great black-backed gulls. As in most predator-prey relationships, it is the slow, weak or injured individuals that are taken first and this helps to strengthen the strain. A fully fit rabbit is not the easiest prey to catch. In full flight they can radically change direction without warning. This high-speed jinking is difficult to follow closely, even for an aerial hunter. When chased, a rabbit will always try to zigzag its way back to the safety of the warren.

Whilst the number of rabbits is partially controlled by predators, the reverse is also true. In good years of rabbit breeding, when the weather is mild and growing conditions are favourable, the predator reproduction rate increases to make full use of their increased food supply. Identical fluctuations in the breeding success of rabbits can be seen in predators. Following myxomatosis and the subsequent crash of rabbit numbers, there was a considerable drop in the number of buzzards hatched over much of their range, until the species learned to take other food.

However, man is the main predator. Rabbits are an agricultural pest and are killed either by landowners or by control specialists. In addition to culling because of the damage they cause, in some rural areas rabbits are an important and cheap source of protein.

A good marksman with a shotgun can bag several dozen rabbits in a day. Snares are used as a time-saving alternative. Loops of fine wire are left near warren entrances or along well used paths. When the rabbit passes through, the snare tightens like a noose and the rabbit cannot escape. Ferreting is a popular and cheap way of hunting. Nets are pegged securely around all the warren entrance holes and a trained ferret is released underground. Sensing this powerful and dangerous predator, the rabbits bolt out of the warren, are caught in the nets and killed by dogs or shot. Expert ferreters can clear entire warrens very successfully and charge landowners for their services, while selling the dead rabbits to local butchers or game dealers.

Behaviour

Like all colonial species, rabbits have well defined social and behavioural patterns that are recognised by and stimulate other members of the group. Basic traits are common to all but some are dependent upon the habitat and social rank of the individual. All rabbit life and behaviour is centred around the warren. This is a random series of underground tunnels, dens and bolt holes that provide safe refuge and dry breeding quarters. Tunnel digging is carried out exclusively by the female. She digs with rapid scraping movements of the front feet and the loose soil is pushed away by the hind legs. Any intrusive roots are chewed through and totally removed. The bucks are often present during excavation but they merely watch or spend a few seconds scraping at the ground. The shape and size of the tunnel complex is dictated to a large extent by soil and geographical conditions. Warrens in sand dunes are extensive with no overcrowding problems. The loose medium and lack of obstacles make tunnel excavation easy. But warrens in chalky soil, which is much harder, are difficult to extend and the number of rabbits per square metre is higher, causing some overcrowding.

There can be as many as thirty rabbits in a single warren, with two distinct hierarchies: male and female. Social status is established through mock fighting when young. This determines which rabbits are strongest and most aggressive. Rabbits tend to pair off with mates of a similar status and the highest-ranking couple, the dominant pair in the warren, sleep and breed in the very centre of the complex. This is the safest place as raiders will attack the first rabbits they find on the edges of the warren. Middle-ranking rabbits surround the dominant pair and the lowest-status animals are confined to the warren edge. In overcrowded warrens the weakest rabbits are occasionally pushed out altogether and seldom live for long.

Bucks have dominance over does but there is little aggression between the two. Fighting takes place only between rival males seeking a receptive female, or between dominant females driving off subordinates from their selected den. In most cases dominance is passed down through the generations. As a result of inherited genes, the offspring of the powerful dominant pair tend to be equally strong. Their mother has access to the best food supply and thus has the resources to feed her young properly. Dominance is maintained throughout successive generations as long as there are no physical disabilities that prevent the individuals from maintaining position. New warrens are formed when a number of subordinate rabbits are driven away. If the local rabbit population is not already at saturation level, they will begin to excavate new tunnels and establish their own social hierarchy.

Rabbits are normally nocturnal and crepuscular (emerging at dusk and dawn), but they will venture out in daylight if they are not disturbed. They will range up to 200 metres from the

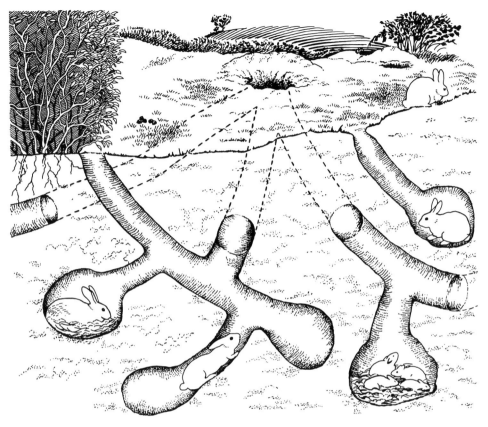

12. *Cross-section of a warren. Each warren complex is built differently, depending upon local conditions. All consist of a maze of stops, dens and tunnels which are interlinked to allow escape if a predator enters.*

warren entrance and will disappear underground at the first sign of danger. Warning is communicated by a rapid thumping of the hind legs, with the tail raised to show the white underside. This audio-visual combination sends all nearby rabbits to their nearest burrow entrance. When rabbits feed, their heads are close to the ground, reducing their field of view. This is a vulnerable position, so every few minutes they sit up on their hind legs and look around. As all the rabbits of the warren do this, they have a reliable look-out system for potential predators. The situation becomes dangerous when a hunter appears between the grazing rabbits and the safety of the warren.

Rabbits have no vocal signals other than a piercing high-pitched scream in times of extreme stress. This is usually used only when the rabbit has been caught by a predator and it acts as the ultimate danger-signal, all rabbits within hearing distance scattering immediately. Apart from foot thumping, the rabbits' main communication is through scent. Urine and droppings are used as scenting posts all around the warren territory. Boundary latrines are left on high or well exposed areas. They contain large quantities of pellets and are found around the

13. *When danger is suspected, rabbits sit upright to get a higher viewpoint for a clear look at the immediate surroundings.*

14. *Male rabbits frequently scent-mark territories by rubbing their chin glands against rocks and twigs or even on the ground.*

15. *During courtship, mating male and female rabbits will keep close together when feeding.*

16. *After feeding, rabbits often sunbathe close to the warren entrance.*

edge of the warren territory. Pellets eventually decompose, so boundary marking is a continual activity. This primarily acts as a warning to rabbits from surrounding warrens, which keeps neighbouring groups apart and prevents unnecessary fighting. The scent boundaries are sometimes crossed by young bucks in search of females. These may challenge the dominant males and in the ensuing fight either animal may be seriously hurt or even killed.

Most disagreements between bucks are solved by non-violent confrontation. Usually a dominant male has only to make a short run towards a rival to make it retract. If the challenger stands its ground, the dominant male struts slowly on stiff stretched legs to make it look larger. Sometimes it scratches the ground violently and then suddenly leaps upwards and sprays urine over the other male.

Once a social order has been set up, it is maintained by scenting behaviour known as chinning. Both male and female rabbits have scent glands under the chin, in the form of a semicircular row of pores. The gland is better developed in males and it secretes a thick yellow liquid. This is rubbed on to rocks, twigs, the ground and even on to females to show personal territory. The chin gland is in use once the rabbit is three months old and it can be seen clearly on males as a yellow staining on the fur. In older bucks the chin hair has often totally disappeared through rubbing. Does also use chinning, but as they are not as territorial or aggressive and do not need to compete over mates, scenting is not an important activity. Bucks are very aware of chemical scent marks and a dominant male will carefully re-scent any mark left by a subordinate animal.

While other males are driven off or merely tolerated, females receive better treatment from dominant bucks. They exercise dominance over the females only in respect of a particular, favourite food. All bucks sniff each doe they come across, to see if she is sexually receptive. During the breeding season the female becomes sexually attractive to the male every seven days or so. At the peak of this cycle, the female is not only willing to mate but will actively seek male attention. Mating usually takes place between rabbits of equal status and, although the male will indulge in opportunistic sexual encounters, the pair will stay together for a short while. During this time, which can vary from several days to a few months, the two will eat and sleep together; mutual grooming sometimes takes place, with either rabbit licking its partner's fur. As the sex ratio is approximately equal, most healthy rabbits stand a good chance of breeding successfully.

Like all animals, rabbits are affected by the weather. It is obvious to any observer that they enjoy the warm days of spring and summer. They can frequently be seen sunbathing close to the burrow entrance, lying on their sides with eyes half closed. Life in the summer months is relatively easy as food is readily available. Rabbits are unconcerned by wind and light rain. They stay underground during storms and heavy rainfall, not only because they dislike water but also because their senses become dulled against the possible presence of predators. Winter is a far more hazardous season. With the onset of cold weather, the amount of energy required by a rabbit to maintain its body temperature increases. The same weather conditions retard plant growth and the remaining vegetation becomes dry and low in nutrients. Thus the rabbits need to eat more at the very time when climatic conditions make feeding difficult. After light snowfalls rabbits will emerge and dig beneath the snow for food. If the snow is deep or layered with ice, the rabbits would expend more energy getting to the food than they could replace by eating it. In these conditions the animals will stay inside the warren until hunger drives them out, weak and susceptible to disease or predators. Mortality rises sharply during the winter months, especially amongst first-year rabbits, but this ensures that only the fittest are left to breed in the spring.

Rabbit population levels fluctuate considerably. The density can vary from two to thirty animals per hectare. The most densely populated areas are in the south and south-east of England. High numbers create their own problems, for in addition to competition for food, over-population

17. *During winter rabbits have to dig through snow to reach food. After heavy frosts many die as they cannot penetrate the top layer of ice.*

exposes the animals to coccidiosis, second only to myxomatosis in its effects. Animals with this disease show the growth of tumour-like lesions on the liver, causing eventual failure. Coccidiosis is cyclic in its appearance and effect: epidemics break out spontaneously at irregular intervals and result in widespread fatalities. It is caused by the parasite *Eimeria steidae*. This disease can kill up to 40 per cent of young rabbits during the first three months of life. An infected rabbit can pass up to 55,000 parasite eggs in its pellets in a day. In densely populated areas, once the disease is established the grazing land becomes heavily infected and eggs are constantly taken in with food. Mature rabbits acquire an immunity to coccidiosis but they may act as carriers, passing on the disease to younger animals in which it can be fatal.

Like most mammals, rabbits act as host to an assortment of internal parasites including nematodes, tapeworms and bladderworms. Heavy infestations cause both gastritis and anaemia. Rabbits have also become the prime host for the sheep liver fluke (*Fasciola hepatica*) in areas where farm livestock has disappeared. The fluke is carried by a snail and is usually found only in damp areas. Ingestion and cross-contamination follow the same pattern as coccidiosis. Large numbers of fluke result in liver failure, causing the rabbit to become emaciated and occasionally resulting in death.

Rabbits also have external parasites of which the most significant is the rabbit flea, the vector of the myxomatosis virus. These fleas are abundant on most rabbits, particularly around the ears. Young rabbits pick up their first fleas from their mother while still in the nursery den. They carry them for life, with fleas passing freely from rabbit to rabbit throughout the warren. Lice, mites and sheep ticks are common parasites but cause few problems to healthy rabbits.

HABITAT
Rabbits are highly adaptable in their use of habitats, though they do not like damp conditions or coniferous woodlands and are rarely found above the tree line. They also avoid low land where the

15

18. *Rabbits have colonised even the most unlikely man-made habitats.*

19. *Warrens are often found in hedges around arable fields. Rabbits raid the crops near the field edge but rarely venture into the centre. They do not like being exposed far from the safety of the warren.*

20. *Before leaving the warren rabbits carefully test the air for danger signals.*

21. *Rabbits can be a nuisance in vegetable gardens. They are very persistent and the only successful deterrent is a rabbit-proof fence.*

vegetation is dense. Rabbits prefer loose, well drained soil with some form of cover other than the warren, such as dense scrub or rocks. The ideal habitat consists of small arable or pasture fields surrounded by hedgerows. As intensive agriculture erodes this type of farmland rabbits are beginning to exploit other habitats.

Sand dunes have always been a favoured habitat; excavation is simple but the loose-packed sand is prone to collapse. The disadvantage is that dunes support a much lower diversity of plant life than agricultural land and, because of the restricted food supply, the density of rabbits per hectare is generally lower. Sand-dune warrens tend to cover a larger area, with entrances well separated, allowing access to more food within their safe grazing range.

Man has created a series of interconnecting linear habitats that attract a wide variety of wildlife. Many railways, roads and canals have stretches of embankment that are left largely undisturbed. These verges are seldom sprayed or mown intensively and still retain a semblance of the wide diversity of flora that used to be found everywhere. Once the rabbits have learned to accept the noise and vibration caused by the passing machinery, these environments make good alternatives to their traditional homelands. Railway and motorway embankments are particularly suitable as they are out of bounds to most humans. Rabbits should be encouraged to stay in these verges as they help to keep the vegetation down, thus improving visibility. These habitats have become miniature nature reserves in built-up areas and intensively managed agricultural land.

Rail and road verges also provide the rabbits with lateral corridors along which to travel and colonise new areas. This may be one explanation for their relatively recent appearances in some urban parks. Often surrounded by densely built-up areas, such parks are unlikely sites for wild rabbits, yet they survive and breed well. Urban rabbits are not troubled by many of the natural predators faced in rural areas. Their main enemies are domestic cats which have become skilled rabbit hunters. Some of these house cats can take half-grown rabbits, but they rarely eat them and the corpses are usually disposed of by magpies and other scavengers. Rabbits are not welcomed by park-keepers who find their flower borders regularly attacked. Left entirely alone, these isolated pockets of rabbits would eventually die out through inbreeding but their population is increased by domestic pet rabbits that escape or are intentionally released. Urban rabbits with black, white, cinnamon and other colours are second- or third-generation offspring of rabbits that once lived in hutches. Not surprisingly, far more pet rabbits are kept by town dwellers than by country people. The slow but steady introduction of fresh genes helps to keep the urban rabbits healthy. The domestic colour strains soon disappear through breeding, although the occasional all-black rabbit does occur in both urban and rural populations. Albino forms are rare on the mainland of Britain but can often be seen in some of the island populations, such as on Skomer, South Wales. Albinism is caused by a recessive gene and constant inbreeding exaggerates its effect.

WATCHING RABBITS

People can adopt the most sophisticated camouflage to avoid detection but as scent is far more important to rabbits than sight they will keep away unless a person's scent is masked. It is essential to ensure that the wind is blowing the scent away from the warren for, if not, the rabbits detect the scent immediately and stay underground. Rabbits always pause when leaving the warren, to assess the surroundings. Their home range is very limited and they know it intimately. Any new object such as a hide will be treated with great suspicion for a few days. It is therefore advisable to build a hide or high-seat a week or so before it is required. The hide should be dark green or brown and well staked so that it does not blow around in the wind. Autumn and winter are probably the best seasons, as dawn and dusk are at reasonable times of the day, but avoid bad weather. In winter rabbits can be lured to good viewing sites by leaving cabbage, lettuce, carrot tops and bread. Do so regularly and in the same place.

Some warrens are strung out and the burrow entrances are well dispersed, making them difficult to watch. When studying a new warren, it is worth remembering that the rabbits will have favourite tunnels which are used more than others. Thin twigs left across each burrow entrance will be brushed aside when the rabbit emerges and, over a period of three or four days, an observer will soon be able to concentrate on those parts of the warren that are most frequently used. Warrens near roads are often the most rewarding as the animals are used to noise and movement from the traffic. A car makes a good comfortable hide providing it can be parked in a suitable place.

RABBITS AND MAN

Foresters, farmers, horticulturalists, park-keepers, sports-field groundsmen and many others have good reason to dislike rabbits. Their presence may mean an annoying minor inconvenience or a major economic problem. To some people, one of the greatest benefits to agriculture was the arrival of myxomatosis in 1954. There can be very few farmers who welcome the sight of rabbits on their land, and landowners frequently hold organised rabbit shoots or allow free access to sportsmen. Other people see rabbits as pets rather than targets. But there is a third viewpoint: that of commerce. The demand for rabbit meat fell sharply following the outbreak of myxomatosis, which is understandable, although the virus cannot be transferred to humans. However, there is still a call for rabbit meat which cannot be met by ferrets and guns, so rabbits are farmed. Although much of the meat is now imported, dressed and frozen, from countries such as China, there are hundreds of smallholders and farmers who rear rabbits as a sideline. Such meat is aimed primarily at the human market, but captive-bred rabbits form a major part of the diet of meat-eating zoo animals. Big cats, birds of prey, wolves and others cannot be fed solely on butchered meat as it lacks the roughage, calcium and vitamins they need. Whole, unskinned rabbits offer a cheap and easy way of providing an alternative to the kind of prey that these carnivores would take in the wild.

22. *Refection. A rabbit eating the soft faecal pellets immediately after they are passed.*

23. *At two days old young rabbits are totally helpless.*

24. *At eight days the eyes of rabbit kittens should be open and they start to explore the burrow tentatively.*

The widespread use of rabbits for commercial product testing is an increasingly controversial topic. Before being put on the market, products such as cosmetics, shampoos and other items are laboratory-tested on domestic animals. Rabbits are used as their reactions are similar to those of humans and they are easily bred. For example, cosmetics are placed beneath the eyelids of rabbits to check for possible physical reactions. The main criticism is reserved for saturation testing, where the animal is exposed to the test substance at increasing concentrations and lengthening times until a reaction is observed. This establishes exact guidelines of safety in which to work but it raises ethical questions and is becoming increasingly difficult to justify.

Food

Rabbits are total herbivores, taking only plant material. They have wide-ranging tastes and will eat a variety of plants, but their favourite foods include cereal crops, root vegetables, grasses and the young shoots of most meadow plants. They will also nibble at the bark of young trees creating considerable damage for commercial foresters; to prevent this, rabbit-proof fences are placed around saplings. Rabbits do not like the taste of elder trees and these are left completely untouched. Strong healthy elders can often be found near warrens while other trees are damaged and even killed by the constant bark stripping. Rabbits are frequent and determined invaders into domestic gardens, allotments and any other site where vegetables are grown. Once rabbits discover a food supply, gardeners find it difficult to keep them out. Conventional fences are useful only for a short time, as the rabbits will quickly burrow underneath. To be entirely effective the mesh needs to be buried up to 75 cm beneath ground level and totally surround the vegetable patch. Often this is economically impossible and gardeners have to accept a certain rate of loss while conducting an intense hunting campaign against the intruders.

Because of the low nutritional value of most plant material, rabbits need to take in large amounts daily and spend much of their waking time eating. Grass and other vegetation contain a lot of cellulose, which is difficult to digest. So that the maximum nutrition may be got from the food, it passes through the rabbit's digestive system twice. This is known as *refection* and is practised by many grazing animals such as sheep, deer and cattle. In these animals the food is regurgitated along the oesophagus, chewed again and swallowed. In rabbits, however, the food passes through the entire system and small soft faecal pellets are produced. These are immediately eaten, directly from the anus. Refection normally takes place inside the warren but occasionally can be observed above ground and mistaken for grooming. The rabbit pauses, sits back on its hind legs and drops its head down to the lower abdomen. No pellet can be seen and the whole process takes just a few seconds. The passing of soft pellets probably takes place underground because the rabbit is highly vulnerable during refection and also because it allows maximum grazing time when outside the warren. The final hard black pellets are left only above ground, not in the tunnel complex. Refection ensures that food is well digested and that most of the useful elements, for example vitamin B12, are fully utilised. Rabbits have a large sac, between the large and small intestines, called the caecum. This contains a mass of micro-organisms which break down the cellulose.

Much of the life of the rabbit is spent eating and this dictates some of the above-ground behaviour. For the first hour after emerging the animals indulge in intensive feeding, which then slows down to a random pattern of grooming, sunbathing, eating and, possibly, courtship. Rabbits close-crop plants during eating and this keeps the vegetation level low, allowing grass to thrive but discouraging the growth of taller plants. Species like gorse and thistle are left alone and, as they have little competition for living space, soon spread.

The density of rabbits affects the habitat, not only because of the amount they eat, but also as a result of their patterns of feeding. When rabbit numbers are low, feeding is selective and they will take plants they particularly like. This keeps many of the coarser species at bay and allows slow-growing plants to move in. When the population density is high, almost everything will be eaten. Grass is one of the few plants that can withstand this type of intensive pressure and in some areas rabbits have converted areas of mixed vegetation to grassland simply through overgrazing. Apart from man and his domesticated animals, no other species has changed the British landscape more than the rabbit. Much of the grassland in southern England has been created by generations of rabbits.

Breeding

Does reach sexual maturity at around three and a half months old, and bucks at four months. The breeding season extends from January to August but may vary considerably depending on local weather and food supply. Both sexes are promiscuous and will mate freely with any warren rabbit but dominant males try to monopolise receptive females, driving off other interested bucks when they come too close. Dominant animals, both male and female, have an extended breeding season which may simply be the result of being stronger and having access to the best food. This ensures that physically superior animals leave more offspring to breed in the following year.

The courtship of rabbits is brief and uncomplicated. It starts with a series of short chases, when the buck runs after the doe. This may appear to be an escape strategy but it is just a ritualised part of courtship. Shortly after this the male sprays urine over the doe, and this *enurination* scent-marks the doe as being the sole property of the buck. When ready, the doe lowers her head and shoulders and raises her hind quarters. Mating itself takes only a few seconds. The rabbits will copulate frequently during the receptive period. Ovulation does not take place as part of a predictable continuous cycle but is induced by mating. This is a simple way of conserving

resources because in times of drought, very cold weather or other local changes in the environment the bucks become sterile and lose interest in the does. Without mating no ovulation occurs. Copulation continues throughout the pregnancy and in most cases the does conceive again within 24 hours of giving birth. There is evidence to show that does can conceive again before giving birth to the previous litter, although the process is not yet fully understood.

Rabbits respond very quickly to changes and one of the most noticeable responses is *resorption*. This takes place in times of stress due to food shortage, predator attack and other traumas. Under these conditions unborn embryos die and their tissue is re-absorbed by the doe's body. This is biologically less wasteful than premature abortion when the young cannot survive and are merely discarded. Resorption means that young are not born into a potentially dangerous situation, neither does the doe lose valuable resources. Resorption is a psychologically controlled process and is governed by the state of 'confidence' enjoyed during pregnancy. It occurs far more frequently in young does and in the early stages of colonising a new warren, which indicates that rabbits become more settled with age and in an established environment. Resorption can be as high as 60 per cent of all pregnancies in wild rabbits and it normally occurs during the first twenty days following conception.

Full-length gestation is about thirty days and, owing to rapid mating, healthy does normally produce one litter per month throughout the breeding season. Rabbit kittens are born in nursery dens inside the warren. Before the birth, does collect grass as bedding and pull out the soft underfur from their chest and belly to provide a lining for the nest. The litter size can be from two to seven and when the kittens are first born they weigh about 57 grams. They are blind, deaf and almost hairless. At that age they are capable of weak crawling only. The doe enters the nursery to feed the young only once a night, staying for just five to ten minutes. Rabbit milk is rich in fat and protein so the kittens put on weight very quickly. They should have doubled their

25. Mating. Rabbits mate frequently during the doe's receptive period.

birth weight at seven days old. At ten days they can see and hear and are starting their first exploration of the underground tunnels.

Young rabbits start to leave the burrow at about eighteen days old but they stay close to the burrow entrance and disappear underground if frightened or alerted by foot stamping. They graze freely at three weeks old and are weaned when the female refuses them access to her milk. At this stage a social hierarchy is established inside the litter by playing and discovering which individual is the strongest and most aggressive. They will hold this social position for the rest of their lives. Under good conditions, in one breeding season a single female can be the progenitor of up to sixty kittens covering first and second generations. But because post-natal predation rates are high a survival figure of ten to twenty is more realistic.

The breeding success of each doe is affected by her position in the hierarchy. Not only is the length of her season affected, but also her fertility. Low-ranking females have smaller litters than higher-status does. Age is also a factor in breeding: as does mature their average litter size becomes larger. However, the breeding response of rabbits swings in the other direction too. When the population becomes too high, the rabbits continue to mate and conceive but the resulting embryos are re-absorbed. Higher-ranking females are the last to reabsorb as they have preferential access to food.

As rabbit populations fluctuate very quickly, resorption is a quick and adaptable way of controlling numbers.

Further reading

Lockley, R. M. *The Private Life of the Rabbit.* Boydell Press, 1985.
Corbet, G. B., and Southern, H. N. *Handbook of British Mammals.* Blackwell Scientific Publications, 1977.

USEFUL ADDRESS
The Mammal Society, Baltic Exchange Buildings, 21 Bury Street, London EC3A 5AU. Telephone: 01-283 1266.

ACKNOWLEDGEMENTS
I am grateful to Brett Westwood for the use of his excellent line drawings. Thanks are also due to Raymond and Judith Wilson for help and suggestions on the text. All photographs are by Michael Leach.

26. *Rabbit looking for food.*